First Facts™

The Solar System

The Sun

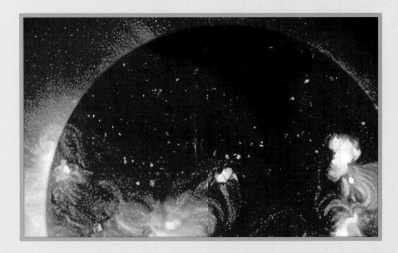

by Ralph Winrich

Consultant:
Stephen J. Kortenkamp, PhD
Research Scientist
Planetary Science Institute, Tucson, Arizona

Capstone *press*
Mankato, Minnesota

First Facts is published by Capstone Press,
151 Good Counsel Drive, P.O. Box 669, Mankato, Minnesota 56002.
www.capstonepress.com

Library of Congress Cataloging-in-Publication Data
Winrich, Ralph.
    The sun / by Ralph Winrich.
    p. cm.—(First facts. the solar system)
    Includes bibliographical references and index.
    ISBN 0-7368-3696-9 (hardcover)
    ISBN 0-7368-5175-5 (paperback)
    1. Sun—Juvenile literature. I. Title. II. First facts. Solar system.
QB521.5.W56 2005
523.7—dc22   2004016444

Summary: Discusses the orbit, physical characteristics, and exploration of the Sun.

Editorial credits
Gillia Olson, editor; Juliette Peters, designer and illustrator; Jo Miller, photo researcher;
    Scott Thoms, photo editor

Photo credits
Corbis/Dennis di Cicco, 15
Digital Vision, 20
NASA, 16; Don Figer, STScI, 21
Photodisc, 1, pictures used in illustration, 6–7
Photo Researchers Inc./Detlev Van Ravenswaay, cover; Mark Garlick, 12–13; Science Photo
    Library, 14
SOHO, 5, 10, 17

1 2 3 4 5 6 10 09 08 07 06 05

Table of Contents

Pictures of the Sun

The Sun is a bright, hot **star**. Looking directly at the Sun can damage your eyes. Scientists use special cameras to look at the Sun. Pictures can show the Sun differently than we see it from Earth. Its surface appears to boil. Its hot gases can shoot far into space.

Fast Facts about the Sun

Diameter: 864,973 miles (1,392,000 kilometers)
Average Distance from Earth: 93 million miles (150 million kilometers)
Surface Temperature: 9,939 degrees Fahrenheit (5,504 degrees Celsius)
Core Temperature: 27 million degrees Fahrenheit (15 million degrees Celsius)
Rotation: 25 Earth days around middle, 36 days at top and bottom
One Trip around Milky Way Galaxy: 226,000,000 Earth years

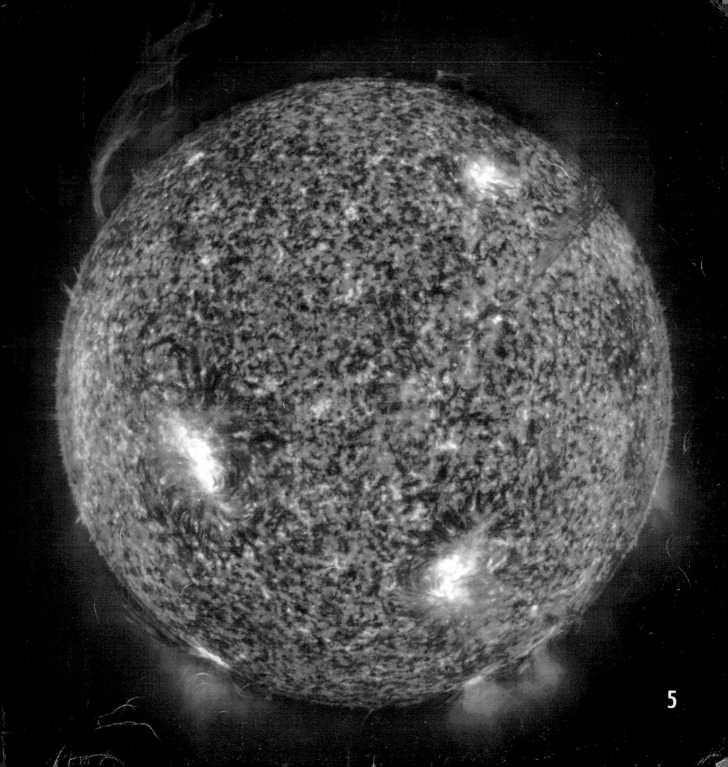

5

The Solar System

The Sun and everything that circles it make up the solar system. Nine planets circle the Sun. Closest to the Sun are Mercury, Venus, Earth, and Mars. Farther out from the Sun are Jupiter, Saturn, Uranus, Neptune, and Pluto.

The Sun is just one star in the Milky Way galaxy. A galaxy is made up of billions of stars.

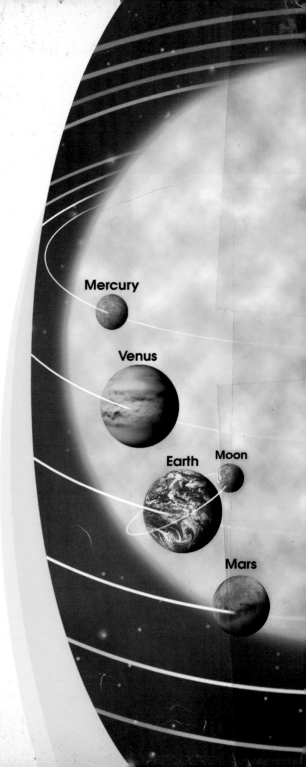

Mercury

Venus

Earth Moon

Mars

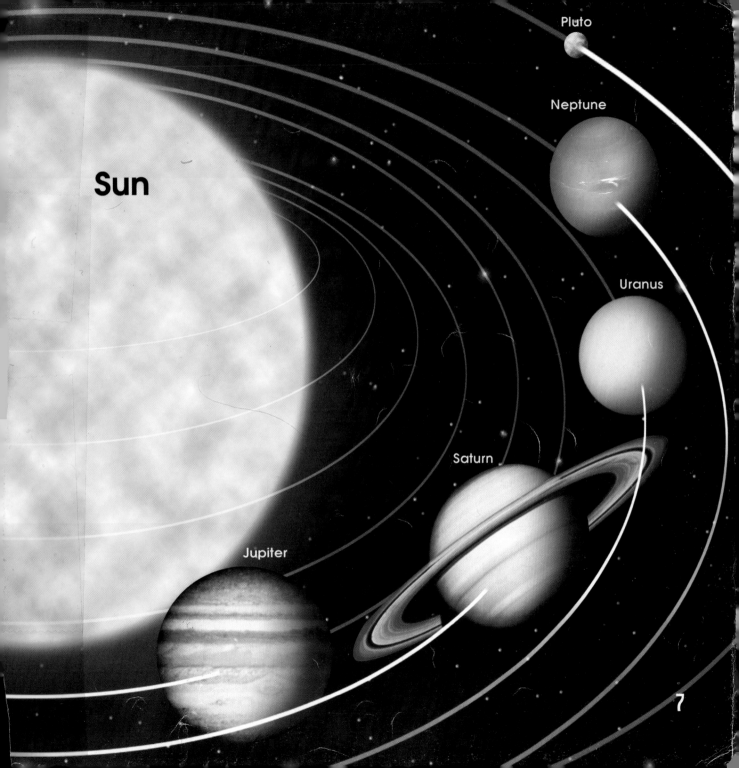

Sun

Pluto

Neptune

Uranus

Saturn

Jupiter

The Sun's Makeup

The Sun is made up of hot gases. The Sun's light and heat are created in the **core**. Between the core and the surface are the **radiative zone** and **convection zone**. These two zones move light and heat from the core to the surface. The surface of the Sun is not solid. The moving gases appear to boil.

Fun Fact!

The Sun is about 4.5 billion years old. Scientists think it will keep shining for at least another 4.5 billion years.

Convection Zone

Radiative
Zone

Core

Blocked-Out
Area

The Sun's Atmosphere

The outermost part of the Sun is its **atmosphere**. It is made up of very hot moving gases. These gases send heat and light into space.

The top part of the Sun's atmosphere is called the **corona**. You can see the glow of the corona only when the main part of the Sun is blocked out.

Fun Fact!

Light moves very fast. It takes only about 8 minutes to travel from the Sun to Earth.

How the Sun Moves

Just as the planets circle the Sun, the Sun circles the center of the Milky Way galaxy. It takes 226 million years to circle once.

The Sun spins as it travels. Its gases spin at different rates. Gases make one trip around the Sun's middle in about 25 days. Gases near the top and bottom spin once about every 36 days.

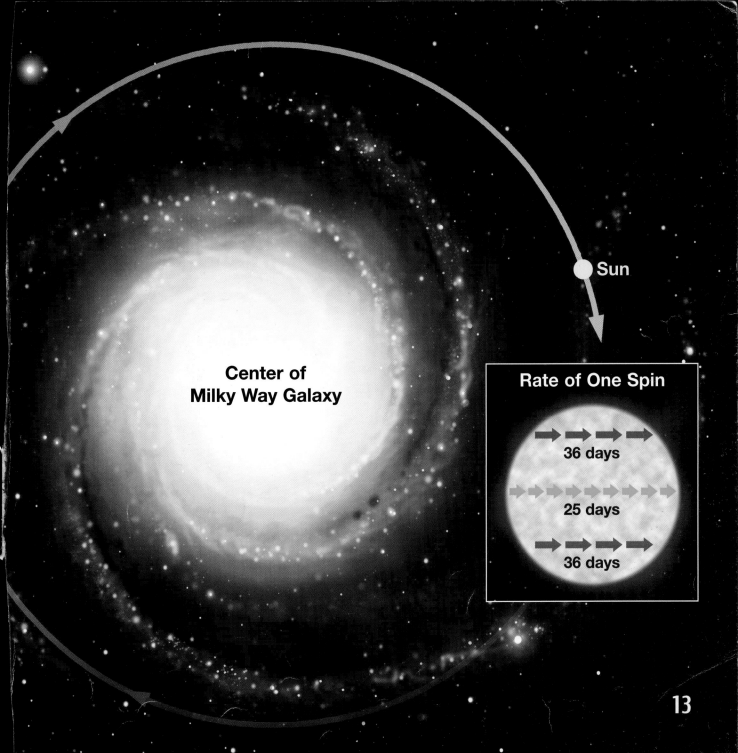

Center of
Milky Way Galaxy

Sun

Rate of One Spin

36 days

25 days

36 days

Solar Flares and Sunspots

A **solar flare** is gas that shoots out from the Sun's surface. A solar flare looks like a flame coming out of the Sun.

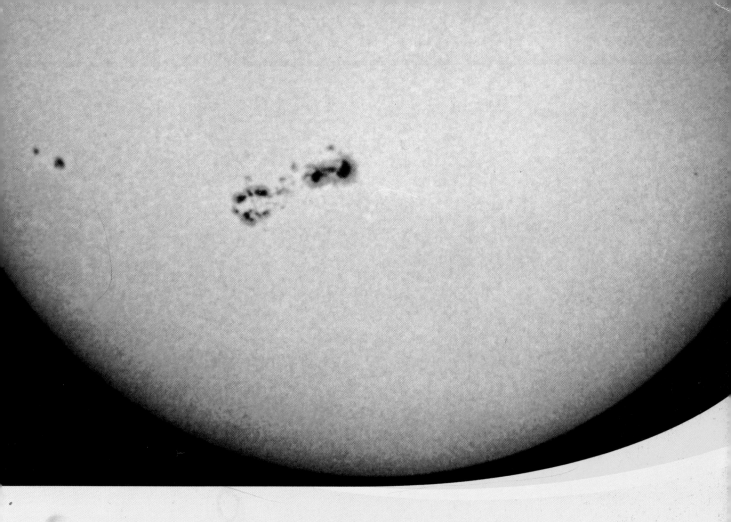

Sunspots are dark areas on the Sun's surface. Sunspots are cooler than the areas around them. Most sunspots are larger than Earth.

Studying the Sun

Scientists use spacecraft to learn more about the Sun. *Ulysses* circles the top and bottom of the Sun. Scientists cannot study these areas very well from Earth.

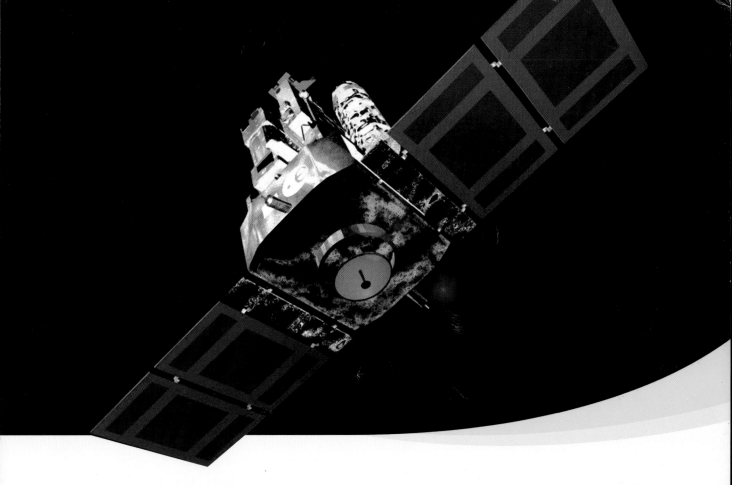

The *Solar and Heliospheric Observatory* (*SOHO*) circles the Sun around the middle. *SOHO* takes pictures of the Sun. It also makes movies of solar flares.

Comparing the Sun to Earth

The Earth and the Sun are nothing alike. The Sun is a very hot star. Earth is a rocky planet. No one could live on the Sun. But no one could live on Earth without the Sun. The Sun provides the light and heat that people, plants, and animals need to live.

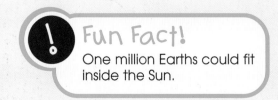

Fun Fact!
One million Earths could fit inside the Sun.

Size Comparison

Sun

Earth➤

Amazing but True!

The Sun is 400 times wider than the Moon, but the Moon can block out the Sun. The Sun is 400 times farther away from Earth than the Moon is. This distance makes the Sun and the Moon appear the same size in the sky. Sometimes, the Moon passes between the Sun and Earth. The Moon then blocks out the Sun. This event is called a total solar eclipse. It lasts only a few minutes.

Star Color Chart

By looking carefully at big stars, you can see that they have different colors. The color of a star depends on its surface temperature. The Sun is a yellow star with a surface temperature of 9,939 degrees Fahrenheit (5,504 degrees Celsius). The coolest stars are red, and the hottest stars are blue-white.

Color	Surface Temperature (degrees Fahrenheit)	(degrees Celsius)
Red	less than 5,840	less than 3,227
Orange	5,840 to 8,540	3,227 to 4,727
Yellow	8,540 to 10,340	4,727 to 5,727
White	10,340 to 13,040	5,727 to 7,227
Blue-White	more than 13,040	more than 7,227

Glossary

atmosphere (AT-muhss-feehr)—the layer of gases that surrounds some planets, moons, and stars

convection zone (kuhn-VEK-shuhn ZOHN)—an area of the Sun where gases rise and fall; as they rise, gases carry light and heat to the Sun's surface.

core (KOR)—the inner part of an object

corona (kuh-ROH-nuh)—the outermost part of the Sun's atmosphere

radiative zone (RAY-di-ay-tiv ZOHN)—an area inside the Sun through which light and heat pass, eventually hitting the convection zone

solar flare (SOH-lur FLAYR)—gas that shoots out from the Sun's surface

star (STAR)—a ball of hot, bright gases in space

sunspot (SUN-spot)—a cool area on the Sun that appears darker than surrounding areas

Read More

Goldstein, Margaret J. *The Sun*. Our Universe. Minneapolis: Lerner, 2003.

Picray, Michael E. *The Sun*. Science Matters. Mankato, Minn.: Weigl Publishers, 2003.

Rau, Dana Meachen. *The Sun*. Our Solar System. Minneapolis: Compass Point Books, 2003.

Internet Sites

FactHound offers a safe, fun way to find Internet sites related to this book. All of the sites on FactHound have been researched by our staff.

Here's how:
1. Visit *www.facthound.com*
2. Type in this special code **0736836969** for age-appropriate sites. Or enter a search word related to this book for a more general search.
3. Click on the **Fetch It** button.

FactHound will fetch the best sites for you!

Index